Emmanuel's Book

Voices of Truth

Children's Questions

Emmanuel's Answers

Emmanuel's Words and Teachings

Copyright © 2016
ISBN-13: 978-1508750260
ISBN-10: 1508750262

Valerie Giglio
gigliovalerie@gmail.com

Acknowledgements

Our thanks:

Teddy Sherwood for typing the initial manuscript.
Marilou Esquerra for her editing expertise.
Rebecca Gurland for formatting.

Pocketful of Joy, for inspiration.
charlottehunter@att.net

PIA Agency and Julie Wright for all of their time and support.

Special thanks to the Parents, Teachers, Young Adults, Children and Schools
that participated in this project.

In 2004, Charlotte Hunter asked Pat Rodegast if Emmanuel would be interested in writing a book for children. Emmanuel agreed and together with Meridith Glabman, the gathering of questions from children began. In 2011 the manuscript presented itself again.
With the blessings and support of Valerie Giglio…..here it is.
A gift of love, appreciation, and gratitude…..

For Pat Rodegast DeVitalis

1926-2012

Table of Contents

I. Introductions ....page 3

II. Emmanuel's Glossary ....page 9

III. Emmanuel Speaks ....page 15

    I Know You ....page 19

    I See You ....page 39

    I LOVE You ....page 59

IV. Bedtime Story ....page 91

Introductions

Emmanuel is a spiritual teacher and loving friend channeled by Pat Rodegast. This book consists of questions that children posed to Emmanuel. It stresses the wisdom of the questioners and the loving responses of Emmanuel. It invites us to Remember who we really are and why we have come to Earth. It teaches us that Remembering our greater identity is the key to living a productive and loving life.

What is most joyful is the mutual respect between the children and Emmanuel. The innocence and clarity of the questions are Heart opening. Emmanuel's answers are wisdom's healing touch. The teachings remind us of our perfection, regardless of Illusion's insistence that we forget our Eternal Divinity. We learn from Emmanuel that we can shed our fears and enter into LOVE'S promise.

When asked:
"Who are you, Emmanuel?"
he answered,

"I am you without your fear; a companion, albeit relatively invisible, along the pathways of Human experience; a messenger of TRUTH, a harbinger of hope; the promised hand in times of distress; the reminder of the greater TRUTH of who you are; the bearer of tidings of good will; and, ultimately, your escort back Home to the reality of Eternity."

-Emmanuel

My first memory of this lifetime is the Lighted presence of a Being who smiled at me and gently walked away. This was at my birthing.

I have sought that presence all of my life and believe that I have found him in Emmanuel. As with all Human experience, I have seen pain, suffering, injustice, and cruelty. When I was four years old I made a vow….that wherever I was, I would make the world a better place for having been here.

I Remember the awareness and wisdom of my own childhood and I respect and hope to nurture the same in the children I am blessed to know. My prayer is that this book will, at least in part, fulfill that vow.

-Pat Rodegast

I first "met" Emmanuel in 1983. From the moment he began to speak, I felt an immediate kinship. As the session progressed, the wisdom of his teachings touched my Heart.

I sensed the TRUTH of his words in every cell of my body. Emmanuel KNEW ME. He SAW ME and He LOVED ME. That hour with Emmanuel changed my life and I am filled with gratitude for his and Pat's "Guidance" throughout these many years.

I hold a dream in my Heart, that LOVE is all there is and to live my life in service to that dream. This book is a fulfillment of that dream and, therefore, now a reality.

-Meridith Glabman

Pat and Emmanuel have been a guiding Light in my life since the 1980's and I grew into the woman that I am with their guidance and LOVE. It is with deep gratitude that I am now able to contribute to their great body of work. I offer this gift to assist children in Remembering who they really are...LOVE.

-Charlotte Hunter

I have been blessed to have had the presence of Emmanuel and his teachings in my life since I was thirteen years old. The purity of LOVE present whenever my Mother channeled was palpable and resonated deeply within me.

I have also been privy to countless letters of gratitude from people all over the world; each one recounting miraculous changes in their life experience, harvested from Emmanuel's teachings.

My Mother, Meridith, and Charlotte are the creators of this sweet embracing of innocence. I am honored to have been included in furthering its blossoming into the world. Namaste Mom; the Light in me honors the Light in you.
     I LOVE you forever,
        Valerie Giglio

Emmanuel's Glossary:

This glossary is to let the intellect know that there are vaster meanings and definitions to Human life than have, as yet, been explored or allowed.

Angel: Who you are without your body, mind, and learned false limitations of Self.

Beings: We who walk with you in Divine Essence and have come to be with you in the name of LOVE.

Darkness: The forgetting of the Human that has been taught to believe that there is such a thing as "not LOVE". It is the fabric of Illusion.

Death: An impossible concept that has become the trump card of fear.

Dreams: The adventures you dear Angels have while your body sleeps that represent private hopes and determinations of the soul.

Essence: The core, the Heart of that which is being referred to; the very fiber of existence.

Eternity: Immeasurable existence that no clock or calendar can quantify. Only wisdom knows the nature of Eternity.

Fear: The false authority of Illusion that has convinced you that you are separate and unlovable.

Forgetting: The noble willingness of the Angel to embrace the world of Illusion as though it is real.

God: The word that mind has chosen to describe and encapsulate the limitless wonder of Eternity that is you.

Heaven: Where the vocabulary of Human longing places Eternity.

HOME: Eternity of perfect LOVE... where you truly live.

HOMEwork: A way to help you to Remember who you really are.

Human: The costume the Angel wears...the necessary limitation in awareness that allows the adventure to continue.

Illusion: The dream you have all agreed to walk. Something that cannot continue to exist unless you are willing to believe in it.

Intellect: The mind's capacity. The brain's offering to the adventure of becoming Human.

Intent: Your dream, your longing, and your purpose...the Miracle you have come to offer your world.

Limitation: A concept upon which the physically manifested world is structured and within which the Essence of who you are refuses to remain.

LOVE: The only thing that truly exists and exists forever.

Miracle: Anything that goes beyond mind's limited capacity to understand... such as yourself.

Mutuality: The Oneness of Angel and Human.

Oneness: The fundamental nature of LOVE.

Perfection: The you that is Eternal. In mind's definition perfection means not making any mistakes. To the Angel Self, there is no such thing as a "mistake".

Remembering: The "YES" in the forgetting that brings Light.

Separation: Fear's teaching that you are alone which creates an unreal experience of alienation from HOME.

Spirit: The perfect Essence of you that lives through Eternity.

TRUTH: The loving perfection of who you are in the Oneness.

Emmanuel Speaks:

I want to remind you that you are never alone. You walk with Angels and there is no such thing as death. There is no such thing as separation from the Oneness. Having said that let me greet you in the name of the perfect LOVE that you are, the Eternity of wisdom that is your nature, and the compassion that called you again to the Human world.

Each of you holds a dream. Each one of you holds a vaster knowing of who you are and why you have come. You have come to bring the Light into the darkness, the Remembering into the forgetting. You are not victims of circumstance. You are creators of Eternity.

LOVE calls you to enter into a very small body at birth. The process of orientation continues through growing and forgetting.

"Forgetting what?" You ask.

Forgetting who you really are; that you are an Angel of Light; forgetting the Divine purpose for which you've come. When I say Divine, I mean TRUTH, Light, and transformation into the perfection of your loving. That is who you are.

Intellect will ask how do I wear that? How do I allow myself to become the perfection that I know I am without being accused of egocentricity, and without causing people to make judgments?

Is it simple to walk on the Earth knowing you're an Angel? Yes and no. It is in those wondrous free moments when you say "YES" that move you into the celebration of Self. It is the means by which TRUTH can be experienced, the means by which Heaven and Earth can be brought together and that is why you have come.

Everyone has a dream and the elements of the dream may not seem to be compatible with your world. What you hold as your longing is your purpose for being here. Give it permission to change as you grow and mature. The Essence of your dream is who you are.

Explore your dreams. Let nothing hold you back. Do not insist that they become what you think you want now. Intellect cannot conceive what the Heart already knows. The mission of your lives is to assist the mind to honor the Heart, not the other way around. Let the intellect, which is essential, be the servant of the dream. Your world has had it confused for a very long time.

So, the most important thing is, "What is your dream?" not, "How will I do it?" Write down your dreams. Every physically manifested Being must dream. How else are you going to stay in alignment with the Divine Self if you don't allow your dreams? Do that and you might be amazed at how many Miracles are created.

Children have enormous questions. They have not yet been taught to limit thought into segments.

When I speak, I speak to the child within:

I KNOW YOU. I SEE YOU. I LOVE YOU...

I Know You

Every Human Being feels unknown, unseen and unheard. You all walk in heartbreaking loneliness.

These questions speak to the wonder and curiosity of the child's dreams and the Heart's longing to Remember.

Justin, 11 years: How was the Earth created?

Earth was created by a group of Angels convening in Heaven who decided to take a trip into an area where perfect LOVE seemed not to exist.

Erin, 7 years: How did the world get here?

We all created it by wanting to serve a greater reality of perfect LOVE.

Ask yourself: What part of the world did I create?

Logan, 7 years: How big is the world?

As big as you want it to be.

Louise, 7 years: How are people made?

They are not made. They just are. They are created by perfect LOVE.

Erin, 7 years: How did the first woman get here?

On the fastest wish possible.

Logan, 7 years: Why are people black?

For Self-identity and for the beauty and glory of variation. Why are some flowers lavender or red? Is this part of the costume? Yes!

Ask yourself: What costume do I wear?

Logan, 7 years: Why do we have colors?

You wanted to bring the perfect Light of Eternity and hold it in the world of Illusion. But because Illusion believes in fragmentation, the perfect Light of TRUTH represents itself in different colors.

Logan, 7 years: Why do we have smells?

We had to fill the emptiness of Illusion with something, did we not? It is a means of identification and aids your understanding of the Human world. Smell is a wondrous means of communication. It is an experience and not a thought; therefore smell holds an opportunity for a greater TRUTH.

Logan, 7 years: How come there are 26 letters in our alphabet and they make so many words?

Because something wants and needs to be communicated. Therefore, to utilize the 26 letters allows for a greater expression of what is needed. It allows more detail and more room for confusion.

Logan, 7 years: Why do we have names for things?

In order to refer to the countless pieces of seemingly fragmented Oneness.

Logan, 7 years: What happens inside a seed?

LOVE whispers to itself and then there is the Miracle of life.

HOMEwork: Why not plant a seed today?

Logan, 7 years: How do roses grow?

With the Essence of sweetness, as do all things, including people. Even when you have become adult and believe you have forgotten, if for one moment you really had forgotten, you would no longer be on the planet. The purpose for coming is to Remember who you are.   That is the gift. That is the blessing. That is the Miracle.

Ask yourself: What have I forgotten?

Logan, 7 years: Why are the clouds soft?

Because they enjoy the delight of non-rigidity and they serve best, as you do, by respecting their own selves. Are they conscious? Yes, they are. Every atom holds the wisdom of Eternity. Nothing is separate from the Oneness.

Simone, 10 years: Where do the birds come from?

They come from you because if you didn't want them here they would never have been created.

Ask yourself: What else do I want to create?

Mimi, 9 years: I wonder what my bird is saying to me.

Your bird is saying what all creatures are saying. Your bird is saying I LOVE you. Pets would not be here if LOVE hadn't called them and neither would you!

HOMEwork: Listen to what your pet is saying today.

Erin, 7 years: Why can't birds talk like people?

Because they don't want to. Animals came to hold Remembering. You came to embrace forgetting. All creations hold the Light. How else could your planet survive?

Logan, 7 years: How come when you are old you have wrinkles on your face?

Because your body becomes tired having to stand up to the false belief in time. If you didn't believe in time, nothing would have an effect on your body.

Erin, 7 years: Why can't people invent a place that you can go to like when you dream?

Your dreams take you to memories of HOME and so the place already exists. You just have trouble finding it on Earth when you are not sleeping.

HOMEwork: What are your dreams when you are not sleeping?

Mimi, 9 years: I dreamed about a place that had no rain, no snow and it stayed beautiful. Is this real?

Yes it is. It exists in your Loving Heart.

Mimi, 9 years: Is there darkness?

It depends what you mean by darkness. All Light it is made more beautiful in contrast to something that is willing to dim its own brilliance. Then the Light can really be seen.

Carli, 17 years: Are there other Beings of Light that don't exist on this planet?

Yes, there are. As the arms of curiosity and the capacity to fulfill that curiosity continues to be developed, there will be a discovery that there really is evidence of life on other planets. As the capacity to reach further and to perceive continues, there will be more discoveries.

Rachel 14 years: Do you believe that Humans are the only intelligent forms of life?

No, absolutely not. Everything without exception holds intelligence – a blade of grass as well as a grain of sand.

Ask yourself: What else holds intelligence?

Jenny 14 years: I can't help but wonder about elves, dragons, unicorns, and mystical creatures if they are real and, if so, where are they?

Dear One, since LOVE creates all things and nothing exists that is not of the Essence of this loving, then the mystical creatures that you wonder about are alive and well in your own Heart. Is that real? Yes. Far more real than anything that poses in physical manifestation but fails to touch your Heart. Life calls you to faith, not logic. To absolute and Eternal LOVE, not suspicion. Do not allow fear to break your Heart. What you wonder about and hope for are memories of the greater reality, alive and well within your Angel Self. Forget-me-nots from HOME, so that the door between Heaven and Earth can remain slightly open.

Ask yourself: What do I hope is real?

Austin, 7 years: How did the dinosaurs come alive?

There was a wish, a call, a purpose and an adventure. When the adventure was fulfilled, they returned HOME.

Jenny, 14 years: What happened to the animals that are extinct?

They have moved to another form, perhaps that loving consciousness has decided to become a pelican, or an elephant, or even, perhaps a dear Human Being. Remember this above all else, LOVE cannot lose itself nor defile itself. The Essence of all things is one Eternal reality, no matter what form it takes.

Agah, 6 years: Is there a really a Santa Claus?

The image is not real but the joy and the generosity and celebration is.

Steve, 20 years: Was Jesus a hippie?

He was a free thinker, a man of infinite memory and enormous Human courage. Did he obey the strict thought patterns of that time? No, he did not. Therefore, if said with infinite LOVE, yes.

Kali, 7 years: Why do things break and die?

They only seem to because, Dearest Ones, you have forgotten the melody of Oneness.

Mollie, 15 years: Is there an afterlife? Every religion questions that.

Yes, absolutely, without question, you are Eternal. I promise you that. Be patient with your world. Fear suffers greatly in its inability to have faith.

Jenny 14 years: Is the Kingdom of Heaven alive?

More alive than anything you can imagine while you are still on Earth. It is perfect LOVE dancing to its own music, and, Dearest Friend, there is no fear present. How could it not be totally and gloriously alive?

HOMEwork: What is my Kingdom of Heaven?

Emlyn, 6 years: Do you really go to Heaven after you die?

Yes. Yes. Absolutely, Yes!

Jenny 14 years: Is there a God?

That cannot be answered with a simple yes or no. It is entirely dependent on what you mean by God. Do you mean a stern authority in the Heavens that keeps books on your behavior and penalizes you accordingly? Then the answer must be no. If you mean the Eternal manifestation of LOVE creating itself, then the answer is Yes.

Brandon, 17 years: Does God watch over us? He must know a lot about us.

No one walks alone. I began our meeting by saying that to you. You have always held dreams that you thought were impossible. Now I want to tell you they are not. Go back and contact that little child you were. The one who was very sure he would make an enormous difference in the world or would die in the attempt.

You witness cruelty, you witness pain, and you witness despair. You also witness magnificence. Be kind and gentle to yourself. Remember the pain and the horror and also Remember the dreams and your knowing.

Ask yourself: How can I make a difference?

Brittany, 14 years: Who created God?

You did. You see there was a need when you became Human to understand what your Angel Self has always known. In order to give the intellect a means to walk comfortably with the wisdom that Eternity holds in your Heart there had to be a hierarchy of power.

Is perfect LOVE real? Yes.
Does Eternity exist? Absolutely.

Is there a greater wisdom than the Essence of who you are that is in charge of all things? No, there is not. It is only fear that has insisted that you are less than perfect LOVE. Walk comfortably with this.

THE WORLD BELIEVES IN SEPARATION, ETERNITY DOES NOT.

I See You

Many of you have been taught to disappear
to hide your Light. To bring Light into
darkness, Light must be welcomed,
which is the beginning of our purpose.

These questions speak to the Divinity of the
child.

Brandon, 16 years: What did I have for dinner last night?

You did not invite me, so I do not know. There is seriousness to that question. I urge you to maintain not the suspicion, but the requirement for TRUTH.

The world most certainly offers a thousand reasons a day to go where someone calls you. It is imperative that you recognize that you are the supreme authority in your own life. I do not mean that in arrogance or separation. The world will tell you who you are, what it is you have come to do, how to dress, to speak, and even to eat. There is wisdom when you are very young to be obedient. And then wisdom says: "Wait a minute, that's not who I am. There is something in me that wants to speak differently, dress differently, eat differently, and believe differently." These are not the words of a rebellious child. These are the words of inherent wisdom.

Take yourself seriously, with profound respect. Each one of you holds the capacity to know the intent of your life, of your words, of your actions. That is what you are responsible for, exactly what you have come to celebrate.

What is your intent? Is your intent to be in TRUTH? Then the world and universe will honor you. Is your intent to bring the Light, to bring healing, to bring comfort to your world? Then you are most welcomed on the planet and, indeed, you are desperately needed, are you not?

The time for healing is already here. What I am saying to you is of extreme importance, first to yourselves in your own lives, and then to the world that you inhabit now. You come not by accident.

You come because LOVE called you and because your Essence is perfect LOVE. LOVE will call you to every important action and decision in this lifetime. It may not appear as LOVE. It may be costumed as something else. If you listen with your Heart, it will not fool you. Please do begin to listen with a deeper knowing, not the mind.

Listening requires a willingness to be open, a willingness to know your intent. If your intent is to hear TRUTH, you will hear it. If your intent is to avoid it, then you will avoid it. So do be clear, Dearest Ones. The most important thing that I have come to tell you is this: You hold the capacity not only to create Miracles in your world, but to converse with the Angels who walk with you as well. No one is alone.

Isn't it time you live that TRUTH? To reach out your hands and ask the Beings of Light who are with you to touch you; to ask and receive an answer; to weep and be comforted; to believe you are lost and be guided. No one walks alone.

I say this to you not because you are frightened children but because you are responsible Beings of Light.

YOU HAVE COME NOT ONLY TO KNOW THIS BUT ALSO TO ULTIMATELY TEACH IT.

HOMEwork: Have a conversation with your Angels. What do they say?

Jesse, 11 years: What is the meaning of life?

The meaning of life is LOVE. It is not the responsibility of satisfying your mind. You came because LOVE called you to be here and you follow that call because LOVE is who you are. You have come to forget and to Remember what I have just said and to worship the Miracle of living when you allow yourself to do so.

HOMEwork: List three things I have forgotten.

Nikki, 11 years: Why did life begin?

Dear Angels, all of you wanted to bring the perfection of LOVE into a place where LOVE seemed not to be. And you wanted to celebrate yourself as well.

Ask yourself: How do I celebrate myself?

Kali, 14 years: What is the purpose of life?

You come to bring LOVE.

HOMEwork: List three ways to bring LOVE into your life.

Kali, 14 years: Why did God send us here on Earth?

Life is not a punishment. It's an adventure, an act of worship, every minute of it!

Ask yourself: Did I have an adventure today?

Joe, 20 years: What am I meant to do?

You are meant to Remember who you are, to fall in LOVE with yourself and to celebrate the joy of this for the rest of your life in whatever way pleases you.

Ask yourself: Did I LOVE myself today?

Anthony, 13 years: Is there fate or do I control my life?

When you say "I," it depends on what you mean. If you are speaking of the Divine Self, you are absolutely in control. If you are speaking of the Human Self, it is a blessing that you are not in control because fear has entered your consciousness and no longer perfectly serves LOVE.

Nikki, 11 years: Why can't we all be nicer and have world peace?

You can. That is why you have come with your courage and your brilliance to Remember. That's why I'm talking to you now.

HOMEwork: How can I be nicer and to whom?

Wesley, 10 years: Is tomorrow going to be a good day?

What is needed is that you take the time today to ask yourself what will make you happy tomorrow? Make room for the answer through your willingness to honor LOVE and respect yourself.

HOMEwork: What will make me happy?

Emily 17 years: Why do we make the choices that we do?

Because LOVE is calling you along a path and you have agreed to walk in its name. You have never made a mistake nor can you ever.

HOMEwork: What are the mistakes I think I have made?

Logan, 7 years: How come when you go to a Ball you have to dance?

You do not, but why not contribute to the movement of the Earth by at least tapping your feet to the rhythm of its movement.

HOMEwork: Did I tap my feet today? Did I dance?

Imani, 7 years: What are you doing? Do you want to be my friend? Do you want to play with me?

I'm doing what I promised you I would do when I accompanied you to the moment of your physical birth. I am loving you, reminding you, blessing you, and walking beside you with profound respect. Yes, I want to play.

Emily, 17 years: Why does our mind work the way it does?

To keep you limited. The mind keeps Illusion alive; that is why mind continues to be honored more than wisdom.

Ask yourself: How does my mind limit me?

Amy, 11 years: Do you think kids should follow their parents' path?

Definitely not. Each one of you has your own path to follow. It may come about that the paths are similar, but the call must come from your own Heart.

HOMEwork: What is my path?

Jason, 11 years: Do kids have more brainpower than adults?

No. Less clutter.

Amy, 11 years: How come kids don't have feelings like adults?

The only thing that is strange to a new born child is fear. LOVE'S expressions are absolutely known to the infant. Children know what the adult emotions are saying; they simply haven't formed the vocabulary yet. When language enters, so does the perception of separation, and the process of "otherness" begin to rule.

HOMEwork: What is strange to me?

Logan, 7 years: Why do Moms get aggravated so much?

They become frightened that you, whom they LOVE so deeply, you whom they called to walk with them again in this life, will not be safe. They attempt to protect you more than they possibly can by directing your actions, thoughts, and beliefs so that you will not be caught off guard by the cruelty of Illusion.

Bless them for that and comfort them in their fear. You are closer to Remembering than they are.

HOMEwork: How can I help my parent Remember?

Dashawn, 9 years: I feel sad and mad. What can I do about it?

You can LOVE every bit of yourself and know that sad and mad are not really who you are. Also, know that you have good reason to be sad and mad. Sometimes the pain of forgetting seems unbearable.

I want you to know that you are perfect in every way and the Angels that walk with you LOVE you through Eternity.

HOMEwork: When am I sad? When am I mad?

Annette, 9 years: How do you live Emmanuel?

I live by the same miraculous circumstances as you do, through the eternal blessings of perfect LOVE, through the willingness to bring Selfhood fully to the present, to wish away nothing and to gather the suffering of the world into endless loving compassion. I have said nothing that you cannot do here now and immediately.

HOMEwork: Where am I compassionate in my life?

Evelius, 13 years: Have you seen God?

Yes, and every time you look in the mirror so do you. Is it not remarkable what endless form the perfection can take? Nothing is not God. That is a very important thing for you to know.

HOMEwork: Look into a mirror today. What do I see?

Brandon, 17 years: How many gallons of water are in the ocean?

Your question is imaginative and confrontational, but, Dearest One, don't waste another minute of your life attempting to receive a meaningless answer or one that you do not have a purpose for. So my HOMEwork for you is that you awaken in the morning and you allow yourself this question: "If there were one question I would ask today, what would it be? What do I really, really want to know today?" Write down the question and spend your day finding the answer.

But know, Dearest One, this question is the most important part: "Why do I want to know?"

There is a capacity for brilliance in your mind. It is entirely up to you how you wish it to serve your world. Let there be purpose to your intellect. Let there be purpose to your curiosity. Let there be purpose to your celebrating of your life. I do not mean that humor is not a purpose. It is. But know its purpose before you begin. The choice again is yours. Nothing can limit you but your own lack of Self-awareness, your own reluctance to be present, and your own fear.

YOU CAN DO ANYTHING THAT YOUR HEART ASPIRES TO IF YOU WILL SIMPLY TRUST YOUR KNOWING, HONOR YOUR INTENT, AND LIVE LIFE COURAGEOUSLY.

I LOVE You

To be known and seen is to be LOVED.

To be LOVED is to be safe.

These questions speak to the child's fear.

Brandon, 17 years: Why did God kill my Mother?

Dear Friend, God doesn't kill anyone. The mind says: "Help me make sense out of the tragedies in my life. Is it true that we are put here alone? Is it true that there is no guidance, no compassion, no sense, and no reason? Is this really the jungle that I have always felt it to be?" No. It is not.

Each soul comes with a promise of HOMEcoming. Each one of you holds the miraculous capacity to leave your bodies when you want to and come HOME. I am not speaking of suicide. I am speaking of a natural process. No one would be willing to begin a Human life if they knew, as Angels, that they could not return HOME.

Your Mother's death was not to punish you, nor to punish her. It was to bring her relief, joy, solace, comfort, and safety. When one leaves the world they do not leave those they LOVE. The only reality that truly exists is the loving. The bodies that you wear are the costumes required on the planet because the planet believes in individuation and separation. When someone you LOVE leaves their body, when they die, they are not gone. I know you felt pain, grief at the loss, and fear as well.

LOVE CANNOT LEAVE ITSELF.

You ask God, is there a higher authority? Yes. It is the perfection of loving. Is that perfection the authority in you? How can it not be? If one thing is perfect LOVE, all things must be perfect LOVE.

That is why you've come to Earth, Dear Friend, to bring those rare and wondrous moments of perfect loving. You hold the capacity. You have already done it and it will happen again and again. Those are the Miracles that transform the darkness, the pain, the forgetting, the agony, the loss, and the despair into the TRUTH they have always been: LOVE.

Each Human Being holds the authority of his or her own life. It does not mean your Mother wanted to leave you. It meant she had to come HOME to be healed. Try to forgive her.

No Angel chooses any experience in a Human life that they are unable to bear. You are Beings of Light and Eternal Wisdom until you enter into the Human world again. You are well aware of what it is like to walk on the planet, to forget, to lose those you LOVE, to stand in the Illusion of separation and in the darkness.

You come again and again because LOVE calls you. Your own LOVE; let that be first. That is not selfish. It is a requirement for becoming strong and present and joyous and wise.

Mark, 16 years: My brother is very sick. He was supposed to die when he was 14 years old. Now he is 21.

May I clarify the definition of death? There is no such thing. You are asking: When will my brother leave his body? When will he be free to come HOME? When will he be away from his discomfort? When will the family be able to mourn, and to breathe a sigh of relief? It has been a long and arduous struggle.

I cannot tell you a date or a time. You are not puppets. You are Angels. You are Beings of Light and it is entirely up to him, to each of you, when you will live and when you will leave your bodies. Is there a plan? There is, and each one of you holds the power to alter that plan if you wish.

Your brother has the capacity to stay as long as he wants. The question is how long is he willing to stay? I do not mean to offer false hope. I am here in an attempt to offer unlimited TRUTH. The vocabulary of the mind says, "If he really is not destined to die very soon, then who is right and who is wrong?"

There is no one right or wrong. He is a Being of Light walking his path and so are you. I would suggest, if your family is willing, that you all gather together and offer him whatever words of LOVE and support you wish to. Allow him to choose. Give him permission to leave or to stay. That is very important because he feels that perhaps he is expected to die and, therefore, he must. Hear this softly. I am not saying that your family has done anything wrong. Of course not! What I am saying is; gather together in a group and speak honestly, openly, and lovingly. Where there is hurt and disappointment, speak to that. Miracles could happen.

Melinda, 17 years: How's Elmo doing? He died of leukemia three years ago.

I know the most difficult thing to conceive of is when the body is not present the Essence always is. How can LOVE leave itself? It cannot and everything that is manifested upon your planet is manifested from perfect LOVE. Please do hear this. When I say perfect LOVE I do not mean what the world of Illusion means. I mean the golden intent of being present on the planet while walking the difficult, joyous, and glorious walk of Human experience; that is perfection. How is he? Joyous, filled with laughter. Turning somersaults and sending you his LOVE. He's still playful. You do not change. You wear your bodies and you take them off. Your Essence never changes! You will always be you. That is the most blessed and delightful thing to tell you.

Tyler, 17 years: When am I going to die?

In the first place, you are never going to die. In the second place, I understand your question from a Human point of view. When am I going to leave this body? When am I going to seem to disappear so others cannot see me?

Most certainly the ultimate decision is yours. My promise is this... You have come to live a very long, very fruitful, very productive life. Mind will ask, can I walk without fear? If only you would; for that is what you have come to teach.

There is nothing on your planet more destructive, more debilitating than fear. I am speaking to your wisdom. You are Human Beings and you are also Angels of wondrous wisdom and Divine purpose.

When are you going to die? Ultimately, there will be a day when you will shrug your shoulders and say, "Well, I think I have had quite enough of this." Then you will lie down and go to sleep. The choice is yours.

Logan, 7 years: How come when you die, you get buried down, but people think you're up in Heaven?

Because, Dear Sweet One, people forget that when you die, you leave your body and come HOME. Therefore, it seems as though the Being is put into the Earth. Only the costume is buried and that is not who you are. The TRUTH of you is Eternal and can do what it wants to do and be exactly where it wants to be, in whatever form it wishes or no form at all.

Carli, 17 years: I want to know when I am going to die. I am afraid I will get cancer.

What is cancer? It is the denial of the Essence of who you really are. Physical bodies are servants of those who inhabit them. Bodies never betray. Fear tells you that you cannot be the Light and the TRUTH of who you truly are. How do you maintain excellent health throughout a lifetime? Fall in LOVE with yourself. Fall in LOVE with every cell of your body.

HOMEwork: Bring LOVE to every cell of your body as you fall asleep tonight.

Ashley, 19: My grandfather died two years ago. I have a hard time accepting it.

Of course you do. How could you not when you still believe that such a thing as separation is possible? You still believe that LOVE can ever leave itself; it cannot.

Nikki, 11 years: Why do people have to die?

Because they want to. They do not have to. They want to. They have been gone from Heaven for too long and they are homesick, even though your Humanness does not know this.

Tyler, 17 years: Will the sun blow up?

No. It will not. Not until you Dear Beings of Light are quite finished with the adventure that you are on. We will then gather and say, "Time for Illusion to return HOME." There will be a wondrous burst of Light as all things surrender to the greater knowing of Eternal TRUTH.

Jenny 14 years: If you are afraid of something, aren't you supposed to tell people what you are afraid of?

Yes, and be very sure that those people that you tell are willing and able to listen. Many people pretend to hear and to care, but are so wrapped in their own fear that they cannot help you in yours. How can you tell this? Listen, not to what ought to be, but to what your intuition tells you. Should you believe that you are truly in peril of any kind, do not judge yourself for seeking help. In fact, demand assistance and demand it immediately. You did not incarnate to be "well behaved". You came to Earth to be TRUTHful.

HOMEwork: What did my intuition tell me today?

Jenny 14 years: Why are teenage girls so mean?

Because they are as frightened as you are and don't know what to do about it. The lessons of how to Be in the world are given from the time of your birth, by those to whom you have chosen to be born. Most people, sadly but TRUTHfully, live their lives in fear and therefore in less than compassionate behavior.

HOMEwork: When am I mean, what am I afraid of?

Amy, 11 years: Do you think that most of the violence in the world is done by kids?

No, it is not. Children learn violent behavior. You are born only with LOVE.

HOMEwork: Am I ever violent?

Ashley, 19 years: Where did hatred come from if we are all from the same place?

Hate comes from fear. Fear comes from the Illusion that you are separate and not in the Oneness and, therefore, alone and endangered, none of which is true.

HOMEwork: Where do I hate?

Rachel, 14 years: If war is about who has the better army, then how do you know who has the better society?

The society that no longer utilizes an army is the one you must belong to. There is no reason for defense. Wars only manifest when mutuality and Oneness are forgotten.

Logan, 7 years: Why do we have opposites?

You do not. It only seems so through the lens of fear's Illusion.

Michael 12 years: Why is life so confusing?

It is not. The difficulty becomes apparent when you are taught how things are supposed to be. If you would allow life to be how it truly is, there would be no confusion. There would only be bliss. The mantra that I would offer everyone is this:

EVERYTHING IS EXACTLY AS IT OUGHT TO BE AND I AM ETERNALLY SAFE.

HOMEwork: Repeat this mantra every time you are confused even if it is a hundred times a day.

Nikki, 11 years: When you're not talking and you don't want to think, how come you can still hear yourself?

Because years ago when you were a small child, you listened to fear and anger from those to whom LOVE had called you. Your inner chatter became the way to shut out the frightening sounds and comfort yourself. How to stop it now? Assure yourself that you are safe….and you are.

HOMEwork: Are there times when I would like to not talk or think? When my inner chatter begins, what am I afraid of or angry about?

Makayla, 4 years: Do you really have to pray?

If you want to get from one place to another, you can drive, walk, fly or take a train. If one wants to reach the greater Light, LOVE, or Eternity, one can Self-Remember, meditate, or pray. Prayer is a vehicle for touching something greater than your linear intellect can Remember.

HOMEwork: Create a prayer that can help touch your Remembering and say it before bed and upon awakening each day.

Noah, 6 years: How can you tell if something is Holy?

The very act of wanting to reach God is Holy.

HOMEwork: Did I reach for the best of me today?

Jenny, 14 years: Why do they have Churches that scare people?

Because those who erected the physical dominion of "church" around the Divine inspiration of Holy TRUTH, though well motivated, were still led by fear. Fear says, "You have to do it my way, this way, or you will endanger your own well-being". Rules were invented and named to be the teachings. They are not. Whatever speaks of true loving, follow it to the ends of the Earth. Whatever honors fear, turn and walk away.

HOMEwork: Did I turn and walk away from fear today?

Agah, 6 years: Are there really good spirits or bad spirits?

There is only one kind of spirit. Spirit can only be good.

Samantha, 10 years: Why am I afraid of the dark?

Fear has already taught you that you have to be on guard. When it is dark, you cannot see. Is this TRUTH? No, Dearest One, I want you to know you always walk with Angels, especially when you are frightened of the dark.

HOMEwork: What am I afraid of?

Jeremy, 11 years: Why are some people born normal and some with birth defects?

It is not meant as a punishment. It is simply a TRUTH that will permit you to walk without fear. As the pain and Illusion of Self in Human form is released, the sense of oddness and alienation is also released. You are meant to walk with compassion as a Human Being.

*YOU ARE NOT MEANT TO SUFFER.
YOU ARE MEANT TO SERVE LOVE.*

HOMEwork: Where in my life do I want to serve?

Rachel, 14 years: What would you do if you could come back to Earth?

Dear One, I would allow memory to stay, laugher to flow, and LOVE to lead me every step of the way HOME.

Naswia, 11 years: What can you give me?

Anything in the name of LOVE you are willing to receive.

Amy, 11 years: When a kid is being abused, is there a possibility that the kid will take revenge?

Yes, of course there is. Are you asking " is that an appropriate response? " No, it is not. If all things were allowed, the abuser would weep and his Heart would break. Fear does not allow that response and so angry reactions can sometimes transpire. But the real abuse is the betrayal of LOVE - who the child is.

Rashida 14 years: Can you help me?

Yes, I can. Not only this time. I can help you anytime, Dear One, that you want me to.

Amy, 11 years: When parents are homeless and do not have money, why don't children understand?

They do understand. When I speak of understanding I am not saying the mind is satisfied. What I am saying is, the Heart stays open in its loving. The Human personality can be despairing but the LOVE remains or the child simply would not have come.

HOMEwork: Is my Heart open?

Carli, 17 years: What's behind the black hole? Can you go through it? What's after the black hole?

Eternity. You all have wondrous imaginations. The TRUTH, of course, is not imaginary. Come on a journey of what cannot be proven in the laboratories and, therefore, seems to be imagination.

Close your eyes and let us begin to lift from the planet, to move through space to where there is a sign that says "EXIT". Go to that area that has been termed black hole and enter it. Do not allow fear in any form to dictate to you what you will find. Allow yourself to simply perceive what it is. There is a portion of you that knows the answer to every question you will have ever asked or you could not have formulated the question. What did you find?

Dinas, 12 years: Have you seen the Christ?

Yes, of course I have but not quite as he has been presented to you. The Being of Light known as the Christ came from the same realm as you. He volunteered to become one of the greatest leaders on the planet. The story is real.

The world is hungry for another messenger of Eternal TRUTH. The teachers are here that can clear the way. The students are here that can learn the lessons.

The mind cannot understand beyond itself, and TRUTH is far vaster than intellect can begin to comprehend. You hold the wisdom of Eternity in your loving Hearts.

What do you want the answers to be? You are not foolish children. You are Angels that have temporarily forgotten who you really are. Everyone on the planet in a physical body comes from a dream of perfect LOVE, and returns to the perfect embrace when life, in physical form, is over. You cannot dream something in the name of LOVE that will not prove itself to you. Nothing is too miraculous. Don't be afraid to dream.

You have been called by LOVE to be exactly who you are. You will complete this journey fulfilling every promise your Angel Self made before you were born. Never allow the voice of fear to cause you to doubt that you are the Essence of perfection in the body of infinite possibility. Nothing can ever be wrong. You are not ever to perceive yourselves as victims.

YOU ARE BEARERS OF THE LIGHT.

HOMEwork: What are the promises I made?

Cherie, 20 years: With all the things happening at this time, what would you change?

Not one thing. The purpose of becoming Human is to touch the world with the Light of TRUTH and, therefore, through the willingness to LOVE imperfection, create a more perfect Eternity.

Anette 9 years: How do you live?

By the same miraculous circumstance as you do. Through the Eternal blessings of perfect LOVE. Through the willingness to bring my Selfhood fully present. To wish away nothing and to gather the suffering of the world into my endless loving compassion. I have said nothing that you cannot do here, now and immediately.

Violeth 18 years: My Mother died. I have no relative, no house. Where can I go?

You can go to the center of your Loving, not your fear. You can go to the center of your Being and say in a loud voice, " I am here". Let those who are hearing you know exactly what it is you are afraid of and what you need. This is a time to develop and to honor the clarity of your Heart and what you will need. You are not alone, we are with you. You will become a true leader through this painful Human experience.

Addendum:

Violeth is now twenty-four years old and has graduated from college. She lives and works in Dar Es Salaam, Tanzania. Her dream is to be self-employed as a rental agent and purchase her own apartment. Here is what she has to say today:

"After I received Emmanuel's answer, I never understood it at first and I was not happy. But after sometime, I contemplated and God's Spirit explained it to me that my home is right in my heart...I will never lack his shelter and constant LOVE. I was motivated to believe that I have a God who cares and has good plans for me. In my heart I planted a seed of faith that whatever good I desired in this life will definitely come to pass......... and this has been so true!"

Emmanuel's Bedtime Story

Once upon a No-time.... there was a gathering of Angels in the realms beyond your Human world. Indeed, your Human world had not yet been considered as a possibility. Each one of you was present as you have always been when all major decisions of such importance are being made. We gathered in the realm of Eternity (Heaven, if you will). There was no such thing as the Illusion of separation. The exact identity of everyone along with their intent, purpose, circumstance and perfection was known to all. In joyous reunion we came together to explore the possibilities of creating a place, an altar, if you will, where we could honor and worship the Light of Eternal TRUTH.

As we sat together, as some of you have already Remembered, we began to say, "What wondrous adventure can we possibly create to fulfill our Eternal longing to serve, to honor and worship the perfection of who we are and the nature of Eternity?"

We began to imagine, as Angels have always done. "Let us create a place that isn't here".

"Well," one of you said, "That's ridiculous, that is impossible. You can't create a place that isn't here because here is all there is." We all nodded with great wisdom.

"Yes, we know that, but there has to be a way."

"I have it," someone said; I believe it was you, over there in the corner.

"We will create what seems to be a separate place. Of course it is not going to be separate. Nothing can be. We will create the Illusion of a separate place."

"Ah!!" we all said. "Illusion, that's the word!" And we began to explore the nature of Illusion.

"What is Illusion?" we asked one to the other, with great excitement.

"It's something that is not!"

"How do we create what is not and have it look real?"

Now, the reason I am telling you this is because each one of you, in your wisdom, found within you the capacity to create something that really is not, and to create it with what seemed to be an undeniable reality. "What was that?" you are wondering. "What did you create that contributed to this wondrous Holy adventure that seems to have enormous reality, but has none at all, except the reality you give it?"

There was a silence in our gathering and we began to whisper to one another.

"What do you suppose separation looks like?"

"What do you suppose something with a beginning and an end looks like?"

"If we created such a thing as Illusion, how would it sustain itself?"

"Would we have to forget who we are and what we know?"

"Would we have to all be brain washed and simply enter into forgetting who we are?"

"That's not possible, we said." "How can TRUTH ever forget itself?" Then we came upon an enormous discovery. TRUTH cannot forget itself but it can be distracted from the Remembering. This was the moment when Illusion was born.

"Here is what we will do. We will create an arena, a sphere that seems to be spinning and floating in endless space."

"Endless space," an Angel said. "I like that."

Then one of you asked, "What are we going to do with all of these things spinning in endless space?"

"We are going to inhabit it," one of you in the front said. " Then we are going to take off our wings and put them aside. We are going to create costumes to wear and we'll enter into the world. We will become so distracted, so immersed that we will invent, if you will, wondrous things that will verify the Illusion."

And then one of us said, "What's the purpose again? I'm forgetting already."

Then you, in the back, responded, "It is so that we can Remember." The purpose is to feel the pain of forgetting, and therefore worship Remembering even more. We are building an altar to LOVE by believing for a very, very tiny while, that there is no such thing as LOVE. Then we will expand and celebrate LOVE through Remembering."

The adventure had begun. Each one of you, Dearest Ones, in this room, designed a particularly fantastic way to honor forgetting - not only your bodies, for they certainly hold enormous distraction - but also some particular point of Human experience. You know what you designed because it has held your attention magically in this entire lifetime. It did not have to be complex. One of you in this room invented flapjacks, one of you in this room created eyes that could see beauty; one of you in this room invented the art of painting, and another one of you the gift of song.

Creativity that is allowed brings Light into the darkness, transforms the darkness, and honors joy. Each one of you knew, being Angels of Eternity, that you held the power of absolute creation.

You were willing to set that aside until the perfect moment when Illusion said, "I've had enough. How am I going to get HOME? How can I be transformed back into Light?"

We all agreed there would be the embrace of perfect LOVE that would transform the shadows of forgetting and the clouds of despair back into the perfection of Eternal Light.

That is what we have done, have we not? Each one of you can Remember your many contributions. Do you Remember when we all decided that we would wear costumes that seemed to insist that we are all separate? We managed, did we not, to create a means by which the costumes, themselves, would find ways to keep themselves alive? One of you in this room invented that very interesting word "alive".

Just then, one of you asked, "Isn't everything alive forever?"

In order to insist that there is no such thing as perfect LOVE, we had to invent something as absolutely silly and unrealistic as Death. Remember?

"Oh yes...I forgot. I'm sorry," another one of us said.

And then the adventure truly began. For, as you are well aware, when an Angel has a Heartfelt vision, it already exists just through the act of loving. Before our gathering had been completed, the Universe had already been created and each one of us set our wings aside, smiled at each other with Eternal LOVE, and said, "I will see you in the Illusion!"

Was it as simple as that?

Yes. We created the birthing process and we all thought it was an excellent idea. We created the Illusion that somehow you didn't know anything because you were little, and the bigger you got, the smarter you were, which, as you are well aware, is still an enormous Illusion.

Here we are, Dearest Ones, and the story continues.

What is it that you created and brought here to the planet? What wondrous and miraculous distractions did each one of you bring? What pleases you the most? What brings a smile to your sweet face? What causes you to laugh out loud or to weep inconsolably? What is it that you hold as your own in this dear wondrous world that we have created together?

Let yourselves rest until that image comes to you. The stars are a part of our mutual creation and so is every little bug, every butterfly, and every grain of sand. They are all Miracles and they continue, do they not, in the name of this Holy journey? They continue to serve by allowing themselves to be created again and again and again.

What wondrous and magnificent work we have all done together! LOVE can begin to celebrate itself by the memory of how it all began. Whatever it is that has touched your Heart in this world, know that it is a promise fulfilled to help you to begin to Remember.

So, as you take your Dear Sweet Selves to your bed and to your sleep, allow yourselves to join the world of Eternity while your body sleeps. Come HOME and visit. We will be delighted to escort you.

You know the way of course, but fear will tell you that you do not, and it might keep you awake and we do not want that to happen. Let us come and bring you hOME for a brief reunion. You still have a wondrous journey ahead of you and enormously important work still to be done. Dearest Ones, know that you cannot permanently come HOME yet. Allow whatever it is that calls to your Heart in your world be your purpose and your way.

Whenever you are despairing or believe that you have lost your way, take a nap. While you are sleeping we will come and bring you HOME for a brief visit. I promise you that when you awaken you will be renewed, revitalized, encouraged and joyful.

The adventure, Dearest Ones, continues through Eternity does it not?

"Good night."

Emmanuel is smiling and kissing everyone on the top of their heads.

Nothing is ever forgotten.
It is only suppressed by the distractions of the world.
One breath beyond...
There is the Eternal TRUTH.

-Emmanuel

NOTES

Printed in Great Britain
by Amazon